A I S H A   D O R I S

6
**WINNING
STRATEGIES
FOR
SUCCESS!**

A POCKET GUIDE TO
PERSISTENCE

Dedicated to the journey of self-love,
awareness and awakening.

Print ISBN: 978-1-63616-249-2
eBook ISBN: 978-1-63616-261-4

Published By Opportune Independent Publishing Co.
www.opportunepublishing.com

Printed in the United States of America

For permission requests, email the publisher with the subject line as "Attention: Permissions Coordinator" to the email address below:
Info@Opportunepublishing.com

TABLE OF CONTENTS

A Note Before We Begin 7

Chapter 1
Changing the Narrative 12

Chapter 2
Identify Defining Moments 25

Chapter 3
Reimagine Failures ....……............ 43

Chapter 4
Prioritize Self-Awareness and Care ....…........... 55

Chapter 5
Persist 68

Chapter 6
Celebrate Every Victory 75

Emotions Wheel 87

Closing Reflections 88

A NOTE BEFORE WE BEGIN

We can do hard things, and I mean really hard things! We can triumph over the challenges in our path and keep moving forward.

This guide will delve into the strategies that have helped me stay on track, and I hope they will inspire and encourage you on your journey. Remember, you are capable of achieving incredible things, even when the path ahead seems uncertain or challenging. As we embark on this exploration of persistence, let's embrace the bumps along the way. They are opportunities to grow, to learn, and to prove to ourselves that we can, indeed, do hard things. With each challenge, we strengthen our resolve and develop the resilience needed to sail through life's storms. Throughout this toolkit I will encourage you to stay focused on the things that matter most to you and to trust your process. Believe you are consistently walking toward the person you are destined to become and the life you've always wanted to live.

Everything you experience contributes to the full measure of the person you are becoming. Your life experiences add to your knowledge, global perspective and self-awareness. And while living these experiences may not all feel good, they all have a purpose. The key is to identify the purpose, learn the lesson, gain the knowledge, and walk forward into the next part of your journey.

What Does This Tool Kit Have to Offer?

In these pages we will talk about persistence, what it means and how we incorporate this discipline into our daily lives. Inside there are six tools to add to your daily routine- each designed to inspire a deeper appreciation for every stage of life. They will provide fresh perspective and insight on how to change our narrative, identify defining moments, reimagine failure, prioritize self-awareness, persist and celebrate victories. We will walk through your story and identify key areas and benchmarks that catalyzed your life. We will highlight your successes and acknowledge the challenges you have faced. We will uncover dormant talents and interests and provide tools to jumpstart your creativity. Your story of persistence is worth remembering. Every high and every low, salutes the tremendous fortitude residing within. I believe in you. Stay focused and don't give up.

Let's take a moment to define persistence. Persistence is a derivative of the word persistent. The Britannica Dictionary defines it as, the quality that allows someone to continue doing something or trying to do something even though it is difficult or opposed by other people.[1] What others deem difficult, persistent people keep working toward. Persistence continues in the face of uncertainty or sorrow. These unpleasant but necessary emotions and experiences work together to form our story, to form the person we are becoming.

One of my favorite stories of persistence is Bessie Coleman's biography. She was the first African American woman to obtain a pilot license. After hearing the exciting rescue stories of battle-worn World War I pilots, she decided she wanted to fly. Despite her passion, however, no flight school would admit her. During that time women or African American students were not admitted into their programs. Although the rejections piled high, Bessie persisted, deciding instead to go to France to learn to fly. On June 15, 1921, Bessie Coleman became the first black woman to earn an aviation pilot license and an international aviation license from the Fédération Aéronautique Internationale.[2]

But she did not stop there. Bessie spent the next two months taking lessons from a French ace pilot.[3] She then returned to the United States to seek her fame as a stunt pilot. Again, she was met with resistance and found no one willing to teach her how to

1. "Persistence" Britannica.com. 2025. https://www.britannica.com/dictionary/persistence (October 1, 2025)

2. Mathias, M. (2024). Bessie Coleman. Retrieved from www.womenshistory.org/education-resources/biographies/bessie-coleman

3. Bessie Coleman. (2018). In Encyclopedia.com. www.encyclopedia.com/people/social-sciences-and-law/social-reformers/bessie-coleman

become a competitive performance aviator. Resolved to learn, she returned to France and took a course in advanced aviation. She also studied in the Netherlands and Germany to receive additional training by advanced pilots. Bessie returned to the States again to launch her career in exhibition flying and became one of the most sought-after stunt pilots in the entire region.

This story highlights four critical points:
1. Sometimes life is not fair.
2. Sometimes people do not give you a chance.
3. Sometimes to get what you want you must leave what you know.
4. You can achieve your goals if you PERSIST.

Despite the repeated opposition Bessie encountered from people in her home country, she found a way to achieve her goals. The boundaries of country, racism, sexism and even the ocean- were not enough to defeat her. Instead, she exceeded all expectations, traveled to new lands and learned the skills to propel her into history books. I admire Bessie's grit and determination. She demonstrated the type of persistence I aspire to embody.

Using the tools in this toolkit have helped me develop the same resilience and stay committed to my goals, even in the face of challenges. This transformative toolkit will equip you with practical strategies to do the same. Within each chapter, insightful reflection prompts encourage introspection, prompting you to explore both inner truths and external perceptions. Journaling exercises provide a rich space for reflecting on personal memories. They offer time to gently explore the emotions that arise and thoughtfully uncover the deeper reasons behind them.

The great philosopher, Aeschylus, said, "Memory is the mother of all wisdom." Take a moment and give your full attention to perceive the wisdom your memories intend to share.

CHAPTER ONE
CHANGING THE NARRATIVE

Speak well of yourself and good things will follow. This is a lesson I learned, after years of negative self-talk. Shifting into affirmations, visioning and empathy completely changed my life. These practices helped me see a version of myself that was previously obscured by doubt and rejection.

The words that come out of our mouth shape our thoughts and influence our reality. It's so important to ensure that the narrative we assign to our lives is dripping with hope, drenched in forgiveness and drowning in love. How do we speak about ourselves to ourselves? Is our internal dialogue filled with affirmation or with critique? Our thoughts and words are powerful tools that can shape our reality. They shape the way we view and experience life. If we walk through life with negative thoughts and unfavorable expectations, chances are, life will feel like it's not working out because we believe and expect it not to. Imagine if we erased old norms and expectations and replaced them with a new declaration of positivity and hope. How do you think our lives will change? Changing our viewpoint is the first step toward changing our narrative. Speaking, thinking and becoming the person we were always meant to be.

So often we ask the questions: What do we want our life story to be? How do we want to be remembered? In my view, the question that holds more value than either of these is: How do we remember ourselves? I'll explain. How do we remember the children, youth, adults we once were. Are those parts of ourselves remembered with fondness or regret? Each phase of existence has imparted invaluable self-knowledge and understanding of others, while also enriching our personal history. Our beginnings rarely foreshadow our conclusions. Life's tapestry is woven with abundant space for unforeseen events: unexpected joys, serendipitous miracles, transformative relationships, and countless other blessings lie just beyond the horizon. Embrace an optimistic perspective; trust in the promise of goodness yet to come. My faith teaches that God has a plan for us to prosper. God wants us to have a good future. He wishes above all things that we prosper and be in good health. I mediate on these truths and allow them to fuel my expectation for great things ahead.

I personally know of the hardships one can experience in life. My father died when I was eleven, leaving my mother to be a single parent of three girls. I did not understand why my father was taken from me at such a young age. His absence was and continues to be felt. My mom filled in the gaps where she could.

She worked hard to make sure we had food on the table. We used to call ourselves Amazon Women! We fixed cars, built shelves, navigated long trips, and did any other task typically designated as "men's work." The women in our family stood together and conquered anything on our path.

I remember being bold, confident and fearless. I remember thinking I could achieve anything, receive anything. All I had to do was ask, try, and win. But along the way, I lost my fight. Life held disappointments that slowly dismantled my courage. As the years went by, I fiercely fought to keep my confidence, believing I would get 'em next time as long as I kept going. My head was above water until a cluster of events shifted me from faithful persistence into doubtful immobility.

I lost my job, my house, my church, and my aunt in a matter of months. Core beliefs were shaken. I didn't know how to reconcile the events. How could I lose so much even though I was faithful to so many. Shouldn't the scales be balanced? I sat in this depressed, doubtful, and faithless place for a long time.

This is the unfolding of my life, part of the beginning and the middle, but not the end. In time, my perspective changed. I no longer carried the weight of sadness. I realized the emphasis was on the wrong things. I assigned my value and identity to my job or perceived contribution to the world. My job didn't value me so

I didn't believe my contributions were valuable. Societal norms framed the warped view I held of myself; that I was behind the curve and a low achiever. Religious communities did not fully affirm my presence. Patriarchal institutions and condescending attitudes toward female preachers were consistent obstacles to overcome. The struggle to thrive in a male-dominated environment is immense, ingrained in biases and systemic inequities. But through it all, I persisted. I knew I possessed a God-given message of empowerment that demanded to be shared. The persistent urging, the unwavering whisper from the Divine, resonated deeply within me, a resounding call to continue speaking truth to power, regardless of the resistance.

Support also came in other ways. It took the form of self-care classes, therapy, prayer and the greatest pep talks from my support system. At times, I would feel an indescribable awareness that I had to keep moving forward. Like an echo from my future self, I sensed an undeniable urging onward with reassurance that I would achieve my dreams. There are times when we are uncertain if we will reach our goals. Rejection and defeat can step in and try to rewrite our narrative. Telling us it is too late, we are unqualified, unfinanced and nothing will work out. But this is a moment when we can use our voice to reorient that narrative, crush imposter syndrome and declare we are qualified, well-resourced and successful. Even in the face of resistance we will keep going. We only truly lose if we quit.

The power of narrative and language is undeniable. I have come to understand that changing the way I tell my story is not just an option, but a necessity for my growth and self-actualization. The words I choose to describe my experiences and myself hold immense weight and have the ability to shape my reality. By speaking life into

> **66**
>
> *By speaking life into my dreams and aspirations, I can begin to see them manifest.*
>
> **Aisha Doris**
>
> **99**

my dreams and aspirations, I can begin to see them manifest. It is not merely wishful thinking, but a recognition of the impact words have on thoughts, and subsequently, actions and outcomes. This journey of self-discovery and transformation is not always easy, and it requires a constant and conscious effort to reshape the inner dialogue. I actively challenge negative self-talk and replace it with affirmations that reflect my true worth. I am learning to view setbacks and challenges as opportunities for growth, rather than failures that define my ability.

This shift in perspective allowed me to write a new narrative that is not limited by past disappointments or societal expectations. As I continue to change my narrative, I am mindful that it is not about ignoring the hardships and struggles I have faced. Instead, it is about recognizing their role in shaping me and choosing to focus on the lessons learned and the resilience developed within.

Changing my narrative has been a journey because I still remember the old familiar stories of defeat and disappointment. I know how the story begins. I know the middle and the feeling of dread as the story begins to replay in my subconscious mind. But now, when I see the opening credits of that old narrative, I stop it and replace it with the new storyline of abundance, creativity, love and joy. These are the new descriptors of my life. I put the old adjectives of lack, scarcity, fear, doubt and unbelief to the side.

Changing the narrative doesn't mean ignoring the difficult things we experience. Instead, it means embracing the reality of our pain, grief, and setbacks while choosing to see ourselves as more than just those moments. We view ourselves as a sum of all our experiences, both the trials and the triumphs, and we commit to consistently telling the story of hope and persistence. This intentional perspective allows us to recognize our growth, our strength, and the divine thread of purpose woven throughout our lives. We are fearfully and wonderfully made, loved deeply by God. We acknowledge all that happened but unequivocally affirm that our best days are still ahead. Our story is beautiful, not in spite of the broken pieces, but because of the way they've been gathered and transformed into something whole.

It's easy to get stuck in a cycle of shame or defeat when all we see are the parts of our journey that hurt. But when we shift our focus toward how far we've come, and the grace that has carried us, we begin to see that our lives are not defined by our darkest days. Instead, they are shaped by the resilience we've cultivated, the lessons we've learned, and the hope we've chosen to hold onto. Each chapter, even the ones we never would have written for ourselves, holds meaning and value. They've built in us a quiet courage that speaks louder than any failure.

Changing your narrative can be applied to your origin story and to daily life experiences. Determine to be your most authentic self in every space that you enter and each person with whom you interact. A misstep doesn't have to crumble your day. Your new narrative is: I missed it but I still made it. I fumbled, but I recovered. I was confused but now I'm fully aware. It can only get better. My life is a field of abundance. The old hurts are now healed scars.

This is your story and it matters. It has weight, and it has worth. Whether whispered in private or shared boldly with the world, your narrative can become a beacon for others walking through their own valleys. When you choose to see yourself as a living testimony of grace, healing, and transformation, you offer others the invitation to do the same. So, continue telling the story, not just the polished parts, but the whole truth. Because in doing so, you remind the world that beauty is not the absence of struggle, but the presence of perseverance in the midst of it.

Congratulations! You just received your first tool. Change your narrative and infuse positivity into daily self-talk. Take a moment in the Write and Reflect section to write a few affirmations and respond to the journal prompts. I hope the tools you receive in the coming chapters will provide reassurance. Persistence isn't easy but the lessons learned during the journey are valuable.

WRITE AND REFLECT

Write down six positive *I am* statements. A few examples are below.

I am fully aligned and in the right place at the right time

I am worthy of love

I am full of wisdom

_____

_____

_____

_____

_____

_____

_____

_____

_____

_____

_____

_____

I believe God has a higher intention for my life than what I am currently aware of. How can I reach for that in the way I think, act and speak about myself?

What parts of your story are you most proud of?

_____

_____

_____

_____

_____

_____

_____

_____

_____

_____

_____

_____

_____

_____

_____

_____

_____

_____

_____

What parts of your story have you tried to shield from view?

_____

_____

_____

_____

_____

_____

_____

_____

_____

_____

_____

_____

_____

_____

_____

_____

_____

_____

_____

_____

What did you realize about yourself that you didn't realize before reading this chapter?

_____

_____

_____

_____

_____

_____

_____

_____

_____

_____

_____

_____

_____

_____

_____

_____

_____

_____

_____

_____

CHAPTER TWO
IDENTIFY DEFINING MOMENTS

Identifying defining moments is a crucial step toward changing the narrative. Each one of us has experienced formative moments that made an indelible impact. There are moments so packed with meaning they have ripple effects throughout our lives. Some impact our emotions while others jolt the mind. They are inherently transformative; and push us forward into a new state of awareness. These pivotal points often prompt reflection; a quiet questioning of our assumptions and a reassessment of our routines, leading to a gradual shift in how we approach life. Such experiences, as noted by *Forbes*, can encourage introspection and a reevaluation of our beliefs, prompting small but meaningful changes in our behavior.[4]

The recognition of these defining moments is a crucial aspect of personal development. It involves a conscious acknowledgment of their impact and a willingness to embrace the changes they inspire. By embracing these moments and the introspection they

---

4. Forbes Coaches Council. "How To Define Your Defining Moments." Forbes, 3 August 2017, www.forbes.com/sites/forbescoachescouncil/2017/08/03/how-to-define-your-defining-moments/

encourage, we can forge a deeper connection with ourselves and purpose. It is through this process of reflection and reevaluation that true transformation occurs, allowing us to navigate life's twists and turns with resilience and an evolving sense of self.

Take a moment and reflect on a time when the unexpected happened and you were forced to react without thinking. Or a moment where an extraordinary act of kindness shifted your understanding of the goodness of humanity. Have you experienced the opportunity to make a truly life changing decision? Defining moments may come without warning. They may be an opportunity to learn and grow, to find renewed purpose and re-examine the original course. Best-selling author and entrepreneur Tim Ferriss says, "What we fear doing most is usually what we most need to do."[5] The beauty of a defining moment is it usually forces us to face our fears and act. These are the things that must be included in our narrative. Sometimes we experience things that were so difficult that we block out or suppress the memory and therefore don't acknowledge their full impact on our lives. Or we experience something amazing but didn't take time to relish in its beauty or importance. We will talk about celebrating successes in a later chapter but it's vital to identify the good times (and the bad times) we experience and acknowledge their full impact. How these moments shaped us, and encouraged us to become the people we are. One of my

---

5   https://www.forbes.com/sites/forbescoachescouncil/2017/08/03/how-to-define-your-defining-moments/

defining moments happened while living and working in Jakarta, Indonesia.

A few weeks before my husband Jonnel and I were scheduled to depart for Jakarta, I began to have severe abdominal pain. I could barely touch my stomach without discomfort. Jonnel insisted I go to the doctor for an ultrasound. The diagnosis was fibroids. After talking to my doctor about my condition, she said I would experience some discomfort, but could still travel.

The day we landed in Jakarta was a beautiful moment. Finally present in the place I dreamed of for so long. The humidity, the landscape and the language immediately captured my heart. I knew I was exactly where I was meant to be. We started work immediately and supported the ministry in Jakarta, trained leaders, taught English, spoke at various services, mentored younger staff, and supported programs for homeless youth. We interacted with amazing leaders who were faced with tremendous challenges themselves. Their persistence inspired us every day. We met with organizations like Save the Children and heard updates about tsunami-affected areas. Our experience there was so amazing, two times, we decided to extend our stay.

One day I was walking and felt a sharp pain in my stomach. The dreaded pain from several months ago returned. I ignored it, but it kept happening. Ministry leadership heard I was in pain and suggested I go to the doctor. I met with the doctor, and he confirmed the pain was coming from my fibroids. He offered to do the surgery to remove them in two weeks. *What should I do?* Visiting Indonesia was one thing but invasive surgery in a developing nation was another. This could all go wrong very fast. We heard the stories of women bleeding out after fibroid surgery in the United States. Was this also happening in this country? Fibroids are often connected to blood vessels and key connective tissue. Incisions needed to be precise. Surgery was a big risk. Maybe, it was time to end our trip and go home.

Perhaps we were optimistic and naïve, but we decided to stay and have the surgery in Jakarta. We knew our time in the country was not finished. There was more to do and this was a part of it. The surgery was a success! The doctor removed nine fibroids, two the size of grapefruits, all while preserving my reproductive organs. God is good! We went to the doctor's office for a two-week follow up, and I will never forget the words he uttered. He said, "Your womb is a ticking time bomb. The fibroids can grow back at any minute, and you may not be able to have children." One success was immediately met with another disappointment. I was devastated. We were not planning to have children in Indonesia, and were not scheduled to go home for another three months. The women at the ministry prayed, my family prayed, we all prayed and trusted God my body would be whole, and children would be in my future. It was one of the scariest times in my life.

I always wanted to be a mother and have children. I wondered if that dream had disintegrated.

We arrived in Jakarta in June and left in November. Saying goodbye to this beautiful land was bittersweet. Our time there was both fulfilling and draining. When we returned home to America, we had nowhere to live and very little money. Our family gave us shelter. At times, we slept on the sofa, on a twin mattress, or in the bedroom in the apartment where I grew up. A few months later a friend of my sister offered us a small one-bedroom apartment in a not-so-great part of Brooklyn. We eagerly took it and tried to steady our lives. Unemployed and out of money, we drained our savings to pay the first month's rent and security deposit.

I wondered how our lives were going to turn out. Did we make the right decisions? Can you imagine this convergence of experiences, recovering from surgery, unsure about my fertility, unemployed and homeless? It was a tough time.

Months after arriving back home a friend reached out to me about a job opening at UNICEF. I landed the role and started work in two weeks. A few months after, surprise! We were pregnant, and soon after Jonnel started an amazing role. Slowly but surely our lives turned around.

I often reflect on that time in my life with awe. What were we thinking? Faith in God's divine plan for our lives was what sustained us for so long. We believed Psalms 37:23 and Philippians 1:6, God orders our steps and He would complete the work He started in us. Today I am fully recovered from the surgery, have two beautiful children, and we own our own home. These are some of the biggest defining moments of my life. I think of these moments for encouragement. They remind me that change happens. Life will take many twists and turns but God will be with us through it all.

I narrate these moments to myself and trust every experience added dimension to my life. Telling the story of resilience, truth and triumph. It changed my perspective on joy and pain, helped me to know that I am strong and will continue to thrive. Remembering defining moments helps us remember our track record of success. During hardship, success can feel distant. We default to survival mode and focus on just getting out of the situation alive. The present circumstance overwhelms all other experiences, and life can feel as if it has always been terrible and will never get better. Thoughts of Why does this always have to happen to us?" or "Why do we never get a break?!" begin to plague our minds. The paralyzing words of always and never negatively impact our view of life and all circumstances. We must remember absolutes are seldom true. "Always" and "never" rarely apply. Life is full of possibilities.

Identifying defining moments helps clarify the truth of the history of our lives and demonstrates we have triumphed through trial and found success through disappointments. Telling the complete story of our "wins" and "losses" builds internal confidence and a true knowing that we can do hard things. It may not always be easy but we must persist.

> **"**
>
> *Life is full of possibilities.*
>
> **Aisha Doris**
>
> **"**

I believe that positive storytelling activates something powerful within us. It plants seeds in the subconscious that nurture resilience, optimism, and a deeper self-awareness. It helps us recognize that a strong, capable, and victorious spirit lives within. Storytelling isn't just a form of expression; it's a timeless tradition woven into the fabric of every great civilization. For centuries, stories have been passed down to preserve history, culture, and wisdom. They connect us to our roots and remind us of who we are and where we come from.

When we share our stories, especially those shaped by struggle and growth, we are not only honoring our personal journey but also contributing to a greater collective legacy. Our words can inspire others to see their own strength, to push forward, and to believe that healing and transformation are possible. Storytelling becomes a sacred act of both reflection and empowerment. Each time you choose to speak your truth, you affirm that your life has meaning, and that your voice carries value.

Don't be afraid to take your place in this rich tradition. Your story matters, not because it's perfect, but because it's real. In sharing it, you offer others the courage to identify their defining moments and discover beauty in each one.

Defining moments can become opportunities for growth because we choose to pay attention to what is happening in the moment and learn from it, work hard to succeed and focus on what is important.

Pay Attention

Life is filled with distractions: social media, entertainment, food, constant noise, and countless obligations all compete for our attention. It's easy to lose focus and drift away from what truly matters. I once had a wise teacher who would always remind us: *"Keep the main thing the main thing."* That simple phrase holds deep truth. It means staying centered and guard your focus.

When you stay focused on your true calling, you begin to move with intention. Distractions lose their power when you understand what's at stake—your growth, your peace, your legacy. Give your full attention to the defining moments of your life. Every step taken with purpose builds momentum toward the life you were meant to live. So, keep your heart aligned, your mind clear, and your feet moving forward.

Work Hard

Growing up, I wasn't taught the value of hard work. Life often felt like it was set to "coast mode," with comfort prioritized over discipline. As a result, I struggled to grasp my true potential. Looking back, I've learned that few things are as painful as the regret that comes from knowing you didn't fully show up for your own life. Hard work has a unique way of revealing who we are. It tests us, sharpens us, and stretches us beyond what we thought possible. It teaches us how we operate under pressure, how we contribute within a team, and how we can turn ideas into action.

Pressure, though uncomfortable, can become a powerful tool for growth. It exposes both our strengths and the areas where we still need refining. Just like diamonds are formed under intense pressure, our character is shaped through challenge and perseverance. I want us to pursue our full potential, to dig deep and uncover every facet of who we are—our personality, our dreams, even the things we've tucked away on our bucket lists. A beautiful life is built when we show up with purpose, work with passion, and live fully

Focus

Focus is about narrowing our attention, sharpening our intention, and aligning our expectations with our goals. It means taking a hard look at what's working and what's not and having the courage to let go of anything that no longer serves the bigger vision. Focus requires honesty with ourselves: the ability to admit when it's time to pivot, to evolve from an earlier version of our plan into something more refined and aligned with our future. It's not about rigidity, it's about clarity. When you choose to focus, you give yourself permission to grow and adapt while staying rooted in purpose.

True focus doesn't just improve your productivity it also deepens your understanding of yourself and your direction. Focus teaches discipline, discernment, and the value of quality over quantity. When distractions fall away and your energy is channeled intentionally, you begin to see progress in areas that once felt stagnant. Focus creates momentum. It's a quiet, consistent commitment that, over time, leads to breakthroughs, greater self-awareness, and a clearer vision for what's next.

Focus brings a greater understanding of your:
- Target
- Timeline
- Audience
- Resources

- Talents
- Time
- Values
- Faith
- Relationships
- Self
- And so much more

Our defining moments teach many lessons. Focusing on the internal and external understanding they provide can help expose the untruths we have believed about ourselves and others. Shutting down imposter syndrome or the negative words from others allow us to better hear the voice of the one who created us. Faith in God's voice and His plan for our lives helps us follow the path He ordained us to follow.

One of my greatest lessons is the importance of valuing my life in the present. I often lived in the past wishing to redo my mistakes. Or I lived in the future, hoping tomorrow would yield better results and fix my problems. Yesterday or tomorrow do not provide what we need to live today. They can provide lessons and aspirations, but to live fully in the present, we need to accept ourselves for who we are today. It's okay to be a work in progress. And it is good to be committed to the process. But what's best is being okay with where we are at this present point of our journey. This is the moment that creates the launch pad for continued growth. It takes persistence to love yourself every day. It takes persistence to end destructive behavior and form new routines. It takes persistence to fight for your marriage. It takes persistence to engage new clients. It takes persistence to present new ideas to leadership and forge new pathways in your company. It takes persistence to continue to heal after personal trauma. It takes persistence to give yourself grace. Each day is an opportunity for success. Let's seize the moment.

Trust Your Process

God gave each one of us a path to walk. Some paths are clearer than others. I envied people who knew what they wanted to do from a young age. Knowing they wanted to be a doctor, dancer or pilot. My journey has not always been clear. My path seems to unfold as I walk through life. All the purpose-filled happenings in my life, both past and present, are filled with blessing but not with all the answers. Purpose reveals itself to me as I flow and fluidly move between different assignments at different times. They are all defining moments which moved me forward. Persistence encourages the realization that there is joy in the journey. Knowing this helps propel us forward in the fight against discouragement. We will win over discouragement if we do not give up.

You've added another tool to your toolbox! Identify Defining Moments and reflect on all you've learned in the next section.

WRITE AND REFLECT

This writing exercise is a starting point to help bring awareness to your defining moments. It moves you forward on the journey of persistence by excavating the wisdom in your memory and the lessons life has taught you. Don't worry if you don't immediately have answers to all questions. Take your time and reflect. Write down emotions that arise if you are unable to fully articulate the answer.

When was a time in life you were happy?

_____

_____

_____

_____

_____

_____

_____

What are you good at?

_____

_____

_____

_____

_____

_____

_____

What have you always wanted to do? (There are no limits-space travel, cook, teach, etc.)

_____

_____

_____

_____

_____

_____

_____

What personal achievements are you proud of?

_____

_____

_____

_____

_____

_____

_____

Describe your childhood. What kind of experiences did you have?

_____

_____

_____

_____

_____

_____

_____

What negative habit have you stopped and replaced with a positive habit?

_____

_____

_____

_____

_____

_____

_____

What relationships have added the most value to your life?

_____

_____

_____

_____

_____

_____

_____

What's the best advice you've received?

_____

_____

_____

_____

_____

_____

_____

What do you wish others knew about you?

_____

_____

_____

_____

_____

_____

_____

What life event has impacted you the most?

_____

_____

_____

_____

_____

_____

_____

What emotions surfaced during this reflection?

_____

_____

_____

_____

_____

_____

_____

CHAPTER THREE
REIMAGINE FAILURES

We often avoid failure. One failure can silence the applause of many successes. The fear of failure can immobilize us. Too talented to go backward but too afraid to move forward. Stuck. It's not easy to share the times we did not succeed with others because failures can be interpreted as a reflection of internal deficiency or external rejection. We do not enjoy feeling the disappointment that accompany failures. Sometimes, we connect failure to our self-worth and harshly depreciate our worth.

Failure can impact our self-esteem and cause us to over-generalize negative feedback, applying it to other aspects of our identities. In other words, when our self-esteem fluctuates, we are more likely to believe failing in one area equates to failure in another area.[6] If I failed at my marriage, then maybe I will fail at my job. Then, maybe I will fail my children. Maybe I will fail in my other relationships. The cycle is endless, and we can begin to believe only the achievement of a goal validates our self-worth.

---

6. Kernis, M. H., Brockner, J., & Frankel, B. S. (1989). Self-esteem and reactions to failure: The mediating role of overgeneralization. Journal of Personality and Social Psychology, 57(4), 707–714.

It is a dangerous road to connect external success with internal value. We are not defined by awards or accolades. We are worthy simply because we exist. God created each individual to reflect His goodness. We are all a part of His divine plan. That is the highest validation we could ever hope to receive. Our internal value should bring the most weight to every situation. The truth of who we are lies within.

What if we reimagined failure and decided to view it as an avenue for insight instead of an instance of disappointment? What if it was a redirection towards your destiny? This is a lesson I wish I knew when I experienced my first major rejection.

I wanted this internship so badly! It was perfect for me. It provided the opportunity to work with faith-based non-profits, and as a bonus, I would get to work with some fabulous people. I saw the posting advertising the internship and immediately knew it was mine. I applied and waited to hear the good news. I was perfect for the role. I was a PK (Pastor's kid), minister in church, pursuing a master's degree in nonprofit management. I knew I had it and waited to receive the call with the good news.

A few weeks later, I saw the company's name appear in my inbox. I excitedly opened the email ready to read the opening congratulations, except it was not good news. I read the words once and then again and then a third time. "We decided to go with another candidate. We wish you luck in the future." I did not get the internship.

I was rejected and was devastated. I stumbled into the bedroom and remembered falling into my big sister's lap in a puddle of tears. She rubbed my head to calm me down, but I could not be consoled. Sadness washed over me. I was crushed. My hopes were annihilated with one email. I failed. I failed at the thing I fully expected to be good at. I failed to receive the thing I really wanted, and I did not understand why. Was it my interview, my qualifications, my personality? What was it about me they did not like? And was it compelling enough to disqualify me? I thought the worst of myself, and I followed that rabbit hole for many weeks to follow.

If I could tell my younger self something in that moment it would be, "Do not worry, you are not limited to this rejection. You are not defined by someone else's perspective of you." I would tell myself to reimagine this failure and make it a moment of awareness. In reflection, this failure helped me become aware I applied for the internship not because it was something I was passionate about but because it was easy and available. Sometimes we have to dig a little deeper to reveal our true motivations and find what we are really meant to do. Excavating purpose is a journey that unearths layers of truth and understanding.

In his book, *They Like to Never Quit Praisin' God*, Dr. Frank Thomas speaks about the power of reversals. A reversal is a deliberate paradox or disappointing behavior that takes place in response to expectations. Jesus was a master of reversals and used them to teach the true meaning of key concepts like mercy and forgiveness. Reversals offer a fresh sense of wonder about old patterns.[7] John 8:1–11 details the story of the woman who committed adultery. Jesus so powerfully reverses the expected verdict and shows love and mercy in its place. He took what everyone thought was a failure and reversed it into a moment of pure compassion and forgiveness. His reversal of the way society focused solely on a woman's punishment helped the onlookers see the inequity and confront their own biases and shortcomings. His reversal of the woman's expectations helped her experience a fresh encounter with divine mercy and grace that affected her core beliefs. When we shift our core beliefs on what we perceive as failure and begin to see them as opportunities for awareness, it can transform our lives.

We are all in need of reversals in our lives, shifting an old, harmful perspective into a new, empowering viewpoint. Things don't always go as planned, and let's be honest: Failure sucks. Working hard to achieve something but falling short can be an overwhelming blow to confidence. Big failures or small daily life challenges can impact our lives and cause stagnation.

7.   Thomas, F, (1997). They Like to Never Quit Praisin' God. The Pilgrim Press.

When this happens its then time to reset, recheck, and reveal. Reset our emotions, recheck our beliefs, and discover what they reveal. Try these reflections as you reimagine failure. Remember to listen and record the words or themes that surface.

Reveal Reflections

- In what ways has this perceived failure shifted my perspective?
- What deeper truth about myself did this bring to light?
- How can I apply this lesson in my daily life?
- What truth am I now ready to affirm about who I am or who I'm becoming?

Recheck Reflections

- Do I still believe in my own strength?
- Can I rise and rebuild from this experience?
- Do I trust that I am deserving of success?
- What evidence in my life reminds me of my resilience?

Reset Reflections

- What might be causing me to feel overwhelmed right now, and can I meet it with kindness?
- What emotion is showing up for me, and what might it be trying to tell me? (Tip: Use the emotion wheel on Page 83 for clarity.)
- What do I need in this moment to feel supported,

grounded, or at ease?

- What can I gently let go of to return to balance?

Affirmations and Exercises

In addition to the reflections implement these affirmations and exercises daily or when you feel things don't work out the way you hoped. They will help to elevate your awareness and instill a deep compassion for every part of your life.

- *Mirror congratulations:* Stand or sit in front of a mirror, look into your eyes and smile. Hold this pose for 30 seconds. Think good thoughts about yourself, your appearance, and your life. Tell yourself that you are loved. Speak with kindness affirming you love every part of your body.

- *Gratitude talk:* Post words, quotes or songs on your desk, refrigerator, door or any place where you are most likely to look throughout the day. Gratitude invites blessings. Thank you is a powerful word.

- *Positive self-talk:* It is not easy to praise yourself when it looks like you have done everything wrong, and nothing is working out. But this is exactly when self-encouragement is most needed. Persistent positive self-talk can help maintain a positive mindset, recharge emotions and level-set personal expectations. Encourage yourself for any and everything! For breathing, walking or just doing the dishes. Our worth and value are not connected to the present disappointment. This tool of reimagining failure will help reorient our personal narrative to showcase the highs in the midst of the lows.

- *Treats:* Give yourself a reward—an extra hour of TV, slice of pie, or long conversation with a good friend. We deserve to be celebrated!
- *Adventure experiences:* Take a trip. Surprise yourself with an adventurous outing, something out of your comfort zone.
- *Sky meditation:* Look up to the sky for 30 seconds, feel God's expansive creation, and affirm your special place in this world. Inhale deeply and realize there is beauty all around and above you. You are on Earth at the right time.

Failure is not a perpetual reality. Failure is not a permanent category. Failure is a temporary experience. We walk through failure to gain knowledge, experience, emotional intelligence, and empathy. Let it be a chance to internally reconvene, allowing self-awareness and reflection to lift you into a higher place of knowing. Navigating failure gives us a depth of understanding about ourselves and others and cannot be quantified. What we learn after the failure is the success.

Congratulations!
You have added a tool into your toolbox. You've now learned

how to Change the Narrative, Identify Defining Moments and Reimagine Failure. Let's keep going.

WRITE AND REFLECT

Write about ways you have allowed perceived failure to affect your view of self

_____

_____

_____

_____

_____

_____

_____

_____

_____

_____

_____

_____

_____

_____

_____

_____

_____

Use this prompt to reflect, write and reshape the view of self- I am proud of myself because:

Ex. I will move past shame because I know my future holds.

_____

_____

_____

_____

_____

_____

_____

_____

_____

_____

_____

_____

_____

_____

_____

_____

_____

_____

Two things I want to say to my past self.

_____

_____

_____

_____

_____

_____

_____

_____

_____

_____

_____

_____

_____

_____

_____

_____

_____

_____

Two things I want to say to my future self.

_____

_____

_____

_____

_____

_____

_____

_____

_____

_____

_____

_____

_____

_____

_____

_____

_____

_____

CHAPTER FOUR
PRIORITIZE SELF AWARENESS AND CARE

At the beginning of the toolkit, persistence was defined by The Britannica Dictionary as the quality that allows someone to continue doing something or trying to do something even though it is difficult or opposed by other people. If I could add a nuance to this definition, it would be: *the holistic engagement of self* to continue doing something even though it is difficult or opposed by other people. This engagement must have the participation of the full self—mind, body, and spirit. Successful persistence is more than action. More than forward motion. It is the successful connection of the full self toward the thing you are trying to do. So often, we are not fully aware of the different components of ourselves. Living life multi-tasking and supporting others leaves little time and energy to take care of ourselves. Prioritizing our mental, physical, and spiritual health is vital. In her book, *Rest as Resistance: A Manifesto*, Tricia Hersey discusses the importance of prioritizing rest and rejuvenation in our daily practice.[8] So often, we prioritize work and professional benchmarks to the detriment of our mental, physical, and spiritual health. Self-care, including naps, imagination, and dreams, are all tools of rest that we can use to

---

8. Hershey, T, (2022). Rest as Resistance: A Manifesto. Little Brown Spark.

help connect the three parts of our self.

Mind, Body and Spirit

We are complex beings, made in the image of God, three parts in one. Just as God is triune, Father, Son, and Holy Spirit, we are also a triune creation: mind, body, and spirit. Each part of the Godhead has been actively involved in the world: God the Father as Creator, God the Son as Redeemer, and God the Holy Spirit as our Guide and Sustainer. Together, they operate in unity, each fulfilling a distinct purpose while remaining perfectly aligned. In the same way, our mind, body, and spirit are designed to work together in harmony. When one part is disconnected or neglected, it affects the whole. True wholeness comes when all three aspects of our being are engaged, communicating, and cooperating.

So, the question becomes: how do we nurture that inner alignment? It starts with awareness and intention. Maybe it's setting aside time for prayer or reflection to care for your spirit, choosing nourishing food and movement to honor your body, or renewing your mind through learning and rest. Each small act of internal care strengthens the bond between the parts of who you are. How can we establish fluidity, cooperation and communication with our whole selves? Consider one intentional step you can take today, something that encourages balance, whether it's journaling, walking, meditating, or simply pausing to breathe. The goal isn't perfection, but connection. When our inner world works in unity, we reflect the image of God and live more fully ourselves.

For me, the first step towards holistic connection was to acknowledge that I needed to communicate with all parts of me. It was something I never fully considered. Each part of us requires attention and intentional impartation.

Communicate to your Mind

I woke up in a severe state of anxiety. I jumped out of my sleep and sat straight up. My husband looked over at me and asked, "Are you okay?" I could not speak. My heart was pounding I could not communicate how I felt, I could not stop the feeling, and I could not figure out why I felt that way. It felt like twenty thousand volts of electricity shot through my body and exploded through the top of my head.

What triggered this jarred awakening? After conversations with my husband and my therapist, I realized I was holding stress and anxiety in my body. Although I thought I was coping well with the stressors of my daily life, apparently, I was stuffing unwanted emotions into the dungeons of my body. I was stressed about my career trajectory, house configuration, recent weight gain, lost friendships, and probably a million other things I didn't want to acknowledge. I was stuck in cycles of over-responsibility, self-denial and striving in so many areas of my life and refused help when offered because I believed I had it all under control. I am so blessed to have a patient husband who allowed me to grow in trust and dependency. He encouraged me to ask for help and trust he would be there whenever and however I needed him. I leaned into his strength and reaped all the benefits of being joined to a supportive life partner. He is a pillar in and for our family. Our partnership is healing for my soul.

I also knew I needed to pay more attention to my mental health and started journaling and processing through daily emotions. I restarted painting and allowed my creativity to flourish. There were solo trips and time to love myself. All these actions helped me quell personal fears and anxieties, move forward and enjoy life.

Lean into the relationships in your life, family, friends or the many different ways your support system may be configured. They can so often provide the love and encouragement we need to renew our minds and continue forward in the next part of our journey.

Our mental capacity is deep and far reaching. The amount of data the human brain can absorb and learn is astounding. Scientists have found each time we learn something new; our brain creates new connections to different parts of the brain. Some scientists call these changes neuroplasticity.

The brain will continue to change for as long as we are alive.[9] Learning, creating and stimulating the brain builds our capacity to analyze, deduce and produce. We must intentionally strengthen our minds so we can transition thoughtful intentions into persistent action. Communicating each day's intentions can take many forms. Some of which include:

- *Journaling.* Chronicling helps organize the day's events and outcomes. Writing can act as a conduit for awareness, solutions and action.
- *Reading:* Learning and discovering new things through the written word helps expand our perspective and supports an ability to think outside the box and live courageously.
- *Daily affirmations and mantras:* Words are powerful. Proverbs 18:21a states that "Death and life are in the power of the tongue." Use your words to speak life. Good health, joy, happiness. You can achieve your goals
- *Visualizations:* Create a mental picture of good things coming to your life. See the image and feel the feelings that accompany. Visualize the next stage of your journey and believe it will be the best part yet.
- *Build a community:* Find your tribe. Family, friends or likeminded hobbyists can become part of a supportive community. Building a support system with those you trust can help us keep going on our journey.
- *Therapy:* Seeking clinical support is such a helpful

9. Psychology Today Staff. "Neuroplasticity." Psychology Today, 2025. www.psychologytoday.com/us/basics/neuroplasticity

tool for mental health maintenance. Therapy sessions are a set aside time just for you. The exploration of the different areas of life in these sessions can have life changing effects. to talk about whatever, you want without judgment.

Communicate to Your Body

Your body is not just a vessel, it's a sacred gift, entrusted to you by God to carry out purpose, passion, and presence in this world. Yet in the rush of daily life, it's easy to overlook or mistreat it, forgetting that our physical health deeply impacts every area of our lives, mental clarity, emotional stability, spiritual depth, and even our ability to serve others. Honoring your body is a form of self-respect and spiritual alignment. It's not about perfection or appearance, but about stewardship and care.

Repeat this mantra with me: *I will honor my body temple.*

How can something that is mistreated perform to its full potential? Make the commitment to care for your body with intention. Schedule regular checkups. Nourish your body with what you eat and drink. Move your body in ways that bring life. What you put in, how you treat it, and how you listen to its needs all matter. A healthy body is a strong foundation and when it's cared for, it becomes a powerful ally in fulfilling your calling.

When I was younger, my favorite foods were pizza and cheeseburgers. They were my favorites not because they tasted great, but because they were the foods I was exposed to. Our dinners were pretty simple. We had a meat, a vegetable and a starch. Rarely did we have a salad or vegetarian option. We ate what was put in front of us, and there was very little room for negotiation. How did you grow up? Were health and exercise emphasized? If not, lets shift our perspective and incorporate whole foods, hydration and movement.

Transitioning into daily persistence means connecting to the mind, body and spirit every day. Tools such as prayer, journaling or exercise are all important opportunities to connect to ourselves and provide each part with a message that we will succeed. After prayer, reflect on having the opportunity to commune with your Creator, and allow this to push you toward persistence. After journaling, allow all you realized through cathartic writing to push you into persistence. After exercise, allow the adrenaline to push you into confidence and a greater level of self-trust because you kept your word to yourself and exercised. Communicate to your body every day. Here are a few ways you can do this:

- *Incorporate movement:* Your daily routine can include ways to get your body moving. Stretches, deep breathing, long walks or visits to the gym are all great options.
- *Nourishment*: Feuling your body with the nutrients it needs to thrive will support a strong body for you to live

in for many years to come.

- *Sleep:* Resting is a form of rejuvenation. The body rejuvenated on a cellular level during deep sleep stages. Take resting seriously and give your body the time it needs to recover

Communicate to Your Spirit

What is your daily spiritual practice? Morning prayer? Afternoon mediation? Evening surrender? How do you allow the Divine to speak to you? Your spiritual practice does not have to take place in a particular location. God can speak to us anywhere. A quiet relaxed location with few distractions is a good opportunity to listen and allow God to recharge our spirit and give direction. God promises to instruct and teach us in the way we should go. God's direction refines the way we reach our goals. His prompts give us insight into the true devotion of our hearts. I recall when I was working on building my social media presence. I started making lots of reels. Some were cool, others were corny. But I liked that I was finally beginning to put myself out there and share encouragement. The reels gained immediate traction and views! I started gaining followers and folks seemed to really like the content. I had a successful day of recording and made three to four really good reel drafts.

I started thinking about ways to increase my audience and

followers. Maybe I should join a social media collective to learn new ways to organically grow my base. I did not know the best strategy to engage with other pages to help me grow, so joining this group seemed like the right idea to offer insight. Throughout this process I heard God asking me if I was trying to grow my audience merely for the followers or did, I have a deeper purpose, to encourage those that need it?

Always listen and reflect on the prompts God gives because He sees things in us that we don't yet see in ourselves. I finally found a group to join but the question continued to nag.

To implement the first phase of the strategy I wanted to connect my various social media pages. In order to do that I needed to log out of all accounts. However, I could not remember the password for one account so I reset it. Little did I know logging out of the account deletes all your drafts! So, all the reels I was waiting to post to increase my followers were deleted. I was devastated. My hard work went down the drain. How could this happen? I thought I was doing what I was meant to do; share my voice with the world. I could not figure it out, but then the Lord reminded me of his words earlier in the month. The prompting He gave me to consider my why. If I had listened, I would not have been in such a hurry to gain followers. I would have had the patience and openness to plan the growth process with God at the helm. Patience would have slowed me down to consider the decision and realize I needed to save my drafts before they were deleted.

Listening to God's leading will protect more than reel drafts. This leading will protect our peace, our businesses, our family, and our lifestyle. The spirit-to-spirit connection we have with God is designed to give us insight. God's eternal perspective helps elevate our finite perception.

Expanding our spiritual ability to listen and follow God's instruction will ultimately expand our capacity for success in every area of our lives. At our core we are spirit beings, and any good fitness coach will say having a strong core is important. Connect to your spirit every day. Here are a few ways to do this:

- *Meditate/Pray:* Set aside time each day to pray or meditate. Use this time to spirit to spirit connection with God. It's a great place to learn how to slow down and listen to God's voice.
- *Listen to music*: Music can be a powerful tool for relaxation or powering up. Whether it is classical, jazz, gospel or hip hop, play an empowering song and let the lyrics stir you with positivity.
- *Read sacred scripture*: The Bible holds immense wisdom. Read and reflect on the divine viewpoint anchored in scripture for your life.

You've gained another tool! Let's keep adding to your collection. Take a moment to reflect.

WRITE AND REFLECT

What are the three positive things I want to daily communicate to my mind, body and spirit?

_____

_____

_____

_____

_____

_____

_____

_____

_____

_____

_____

_____

_____

_____

_____

_____

_____

What areas in my life need the most care?

_____

_____

_____

_____

_____

_____

_____

_____

_____

_____

_____

_____

_____

_____

_____

_____

_____

_____

What benefits will a daily self-care plan offer my life?

_____

_____

_____

_____

_____

_____

_____

_____

_____

_____

_____

_____

_____

_____

_____

_____

_____

_____

CHAPTER FIVE
PERSIST

There are moments in life when everything starts to align, when clarity, purpose, and peace seem to move in sync. These seasons are deeply meaningful, invite us to pause and reflect on how we arrived at this moment of harmony. Are the changes being made to our narrative, self-talk and care having an impact? What are we doing differently to cause this? It's in these times that we catch a glimpse of what life can look like when we're fully present, intentional, and in tune with who we are. But more importantly, these moments teach us that lasting change doesn't happen by accident, it must be nurtured with focus and commitment.

I remember one season where I truly felt the pieces of my life falling into place. Everything seemed to click. I recognized the momentum I was in, and I leaned into it intentionally to sustain that growth. Real transformation takes persistence and not just in one area, but across the whole of who we are. True progress engages the mind, body, and spirit. It's about showing up consistently,

> *Real transformation takes persistence.*
>
> **Aisha Doris**

choosing growth, and honoring the process. Persistence isn't just willpower; it's a holistic rhythm of discipline, self-care, and alignment that helps us grow into our highest potential. As we prioritize wellness and invest in ourselves, we find that persistence becomes the bridge between vision and fulfillment.

But once we've caught that rhythm and things start moving forward, the next challenge arises: how do we transform momentum into sustainable action? The answer lies in creating structure, staying rooted in purpose, and remaining honest with ourselves about what's working and what's not. When we understand why we're doing what we're doing, and when all parts of ourselves are aligned, we can build habits that last. A habit that has helped me stay consistent is the implementation of routines in daily life.

Routines

Routines are an excellent framework to help govern life. They help train the mind and body to consistently apply focus to a particular area. A routine identifies possible goals and targets for the short or long term.

Key things to remember when creating a tailored routine for your life:

- Identify areas of importance and places for improvement.
- Set clear, reachable goals and timelines.

- Organize your schedule. Identify when, what and how to incorporate this structure into your daily life. Rountinesc n look different each day or week. One day brainstorming is the focus while drafting is highlighted the next day.

Commit to your routine. Life always happens, we get busy and overwhelmed, but decide, no matter what comes, you will stick with it. Be kind to yourself. Persistent productivity is what we're after, not rigidity.

Routines should be built around the three parts of self: mind, body spirit. Here are some sample routines. Feel free to tailor them to your specific needs.

Mind

- *Visualization.* Create a visualization routine helps the mind create pictures and assurance about our ability to succeed. The rigors of life can overwhelm our ability to find balance. Visualizing successful prioritization helps the mind manage the days tasks.
- *To-do lists.* Creating a daily schedule outlining daily tasks helps to relieve mental pressure and keeps us encouraged by acknowledging what we have accomplished.
- *Daily affirmations and mantras.* These short but powerful sayings can retrain the mind to think positively about

life and the future.

Body

- *Breathing exercises.* This a good technique for traversing weighty emotions. Emotional overwhelm can send us into a tailspin. Breathing helps settle the body and remove it from fight-or- flight mode. Deep inhales and slow exhales are an ancient signal to the body we are safe and okay. Breathing reminds us we are alive and can endure our present circumstance. Attaching an empowering mantra to breaths is also helpful. Examples are, "I am enough." "I receive peace."

- *Consistent exercise.* Movement is important to our daily lives. Keeping a consistent exercise routine can have positive impact on both our physical and mental well-being. Listen to your body and what it needs. Find a movement regimen to fit your needs. Stretching, yoga or walking are all great options!

Spirit

- *Prayer.* Connection to God is an amazing tool in persistence. Prayer tugs on the Divine Source to act and to give instruction, comfort, and blessing. Prayer can take many forms depending on the situation so go with the flow! Let your heart guide. Surrender and connection to the voice of God are what's most important. Finding a set time to pray adds a simple routine to your schedule where you can look forward to your time with God.

Persistence in action does not mean we impose strict deadlines and harsh requirements on ourselves. It means having a real commitment to proceed, one step, one yard, and one mile at a time. Infusing massive amounts of self-love into each persistent action is key.

I want to encourage you. Although you may have tried to achieve your goals many times in the past without success, keep persisting. I join my faith and expectation with yours. I'm believing for unexpected blessings that will bring fulfillment and alignment with your life's purpose. Let's not allow our current situation to impede our progress toward a new future.

Another tool in your toolkit. Now you have Change the Narrative, Identify Defining Moments and Reimagine Failure, Prioritize Self Awareness and Care and Persist. Let's keep going!

WRITE AND REFLECT

What routines can I create for my life?

_____

_____

_____

_____

_____

_____

_____

_____

_____

_____

_____

_____

_____

_____

_____

_____

_____

_____

_____

_____

What would help you stick to this routine?

_____

_____

_____

_____

_____

_____

_____

_____

_____

_____

_____

_____

_____

_____

_____

_____

_____

_____

CHAPTER SIX
CELEBRATE EVERY VICTORY

Every victory deserves to be celebrated. Small steps lead to big strides. Zechariah 4:10 says "Do not despise these small beginnings, for the Lord rejoices to see the work begin." God is so happy to see us start. It is a gift to receive an idea, brainstorm the strategic plan and day dream about the possibilities.

Every step in the process is important. Sometimes we get discouraged because we had the idea but haven't finished the plan. The ensuing negative outlook often stifles the forward movement. Imagine if instead of condemning ourselves we celebrated. How wonderful to have an idea, to be so inspired to ideate a fresh perspective. Billions of people in the world and that idea came to you. It's worth celebrating. The beginning is just as important as the end.

Celebration helps to boost the mood and instill confidence. It provides a pause from worrying about the next step and allows the body, mind and spirit to savor moments of joy. According to social psychology researcher Fred Bryant and others, when we stop to savor the good things that happen, we buffer ourselves against the bad and build resilience. Even mini-celebrations can enhance positive emotions and make it easier to cope with daily challenges and stressors.[10] Celebration shifts our focus and provides ways to incorporate joyful routines into our lives. Bryant's research also suggests most people do not celebrate the good things in a way that "maximizes their positive effects." There are many benefits to savoring the good things including relationship building, improved mental and physical health, and discovering pathways to creative problem solving."[11] Imagine if we embraced the celebration and reaped all of the glorious benefits.

There's something powerful about recognizing how our mindset shapes our momentum. Many of us begin with ambition and clarity, eager to achieve our goals and live out our purpose. But as life unfolds—filled with responsibilities, unexpected detours, and shifting priorities—we often find ourselves running on empty. What once felt exciting can begin to feel like a burden. In those moments, it becomes clear that sustainability, not just drive, is the key to lasting success. And one of the most overlooked tools in staying consistent is *celebration.*

I've always been a high achiever—someone who thrives on

10. Frye, D. "Why You Should Celebrate Everything." Psychology Today, 2 December 2015. www.psychologytoday.com/us/blog/imperfect-spirituality/201512/why-you-should-celebrate-everything

11. Kennelly, S. "10 Steps to Savoring the Good Things in Life." Greater Good Magazine, 23 July 2012. greatergood.berkeley.edu/article/item/10_steps_to_savoring_the_good_things_in_life

starting strong and finishing well. But when career demands, family life, children, and daily responsibilities entered the picture, I found it hard to maintain the same level of motivation and energy. I was running on discipline, but I wasn't feeling fulfilled. That changed when I intentionally began incorporating celebration into my routine. Celebrating even small wins helped me release the pressure to be perfect. It reminded me that progress doesn't have to be huge or perfectly timed to matter. What shifted wasn't just my schedule, it was my mindset. And with that shift, I found new joy in my journey.

By allowing myself to acknowledge growth along the way, I no longer felt like I was chasing an unattainable finish line. Each step forward, no matter how quiet or unscripted, became a reason to keep going. I began to value process over perfection and momentum over milestones. This shift brought more peace and presence into my everyday life. I realized that celebrating doesn't mean settling, it means honoring your effort and keeping your spirit engaged.

If you're feeling overwhelmed or discouraged, ask yourself: *When was the last time I celebrated how far I've come?* Sometimes the breakthrough isn't found in working harder, but in recognizing that you're already making meaningful progress. When you learn to celebrate the journey, not just the destination, you begin to live with greater purpose, energy, and grace. Your path becomes not only sustainable but deeply satisfying.

What are some ways you can change your perspective about celebration? How can you incorporate joy into your daily routine?

Celebration Routines

Here are a few tips to help you mindfully receive the benefits of celebration:

> **"**
>
> *Take a moment to reflect on the victory and truly be inspired by it.*
>
> **Aisha Doris**

- *Practice awe and wonder:* Take a moment to reflect on the victory and truly be inspired by it. You were the vessel used to manifest this victory- small or big. It's amazing to be a part of the dispensation of divine wisdom.
- *Share the news:* Tell the people in your community the good news. An outward expression of good news can help concretize the victory because it becomes a shared experience, one that is celebrated by many.
- *Mark the moment:* Write it down. Grab your journal and record what happened. Write about it in the best way possible. Don't be afraid of effusive adjectives and superlatives. This is your historical record to look back on and remember the beauty of your success. Mini-celebrations are also a wonderful concept to integrate.

They broaden the understanding of what, when and how things can be celebrated. What if celebrations were incorporated throughout the day through thoughtful prompts and mantras? Reciting a daily mantra to promote internal encouragement could have powerful results.

These mantras could include:
- You did great
- I'm so proud of you
- Wow, you're amazing
- Keep going
- I am fully resourced and supported
- I am here and ready
- I'm participating in the best idea for my life
- Thank you, for everything

Reciting these mantras to yourself throughout the day helps to celebrate victories you may not have realized you achieved. They help focus the mind and ground the body with an empowered viewpoint of success.

You have read this toolkit and received tools to help you contemplate past and present experiences. Use these times of reflection to help celebrate your wins and successes and identify defining moments. Build systems in your life to encourage self-care and awareness so you can maintain positive thoughts and practices. I am so excited you are on this journey. Great things are already happening and will continue to happen in your life. Persistence has always changed the world. Shirley Chisholm, brought her own seat to that table and became the first African-American woman to be elected to Congress and run for President. Maria Curie braved dangerous work conditions and changed the way we use radiation in science. Ida B. Wells was an influential journalist who helped change the way the public looked at violence against African American people. Malala Yousafzai a courageous woman who became a vocal advocate for girls' education in Pakistan, Mae Jemison worked hard and became the first African American woman in space. Langston Hughes, James Baldwin and Nikki Giovanni were all poets who impacted the world with their words. Junko Tabei, the first woman to make it to the top of Mount Everest. These champions pushed through difficult circumstances to see change.

You are a champion. A world changer. It may not always feel or look like it but God has placed tremendous talent and ability in you. Your desire to create, inspire, cook, dance, swim, smile and live is evidence that you are on Earth for a reason. You are individually crafted by God, and He does not take you for granted. Never underestimate your value.

Congratulations! You've added six tools to your toolbox of persistence. Change your Narrative, Identify Defining Moments, Re-Imagine Failure, Prioritize Self-Awareness and Care, Persist, and Celebrate Every Victory! Use them wisely and consistently. I know they will tremendously impact your life.

Stay focused, stay grounded, and keep moving forward—you've got this. I'm not speaking from theory; I've lived the reality of persistence. I've walked through seasons of pain—surviving abuse, navigating devastating career and life disappointments, even enduring emergency surgery in a foreign country. Through it all, one thing anchored me: persistence. It wasn't always pretty, and results didn't always fast, but I kept going because deep down, I knew I was made for more. And so are you. Don't shrink back. Push forward, and allow the strength and brilliance already within you to rise to the surface. Love yourself enough to keep showing up, again and again.

Your journey is not defined by the hardest moments, but by the courage you show in how you respond to them. Through every reframe, every realignment of your mind, body and spirit, you are writing a powerful story of resilience. You've learned to focus when life tried to distract you. You've fought for your wellness when the world told you to keep going without rest. You've honored your story and your voice, learning to celebrate progress, no matter how small. You've discovered that taking care of your whole self is not a luxury but the very foundation of lasting purpose. And in doing so, you've built strength not only for yourself, but for those who will follow your lead.

So, as you turn the final pages of this book, let this be your reminder: you are capable, you are chosen, and your journey is far from over. Embrace focus as your compass, persistence as your fuel, and self-love as your anchor. You are a whole being, mind, body, and spirit, designed with intention, crafted in the image of God, and destined for a life of depth, joy, and impact. Keep writing your story. Keep showing up. And never forget that your consistent, wholehearted pursuit of growth is already a legacy in motion. Push forward and see the radiance of your true self on display. Love yourself, persistently.

WRITE AND REFLECT

When was the last time you were proud of yourself.

_____

_____

_____

_____

_____

_____

_____

_____

_____

_____

_____

_____

_____

_____

_____

_____

_____

_____

What will you do to celebrate your next victory?

_____

_____

_____

_____

_____

_____

_____

_____

_____

_____

_____

_____

_____

_____

_____

_____

_____

_____

Imagine the perfect dream celebration. Include how you will feel when victory happens, who will be there to celebrate with you, where you will celebrate and anything else that comes to mind.

_____

_____

_____

_____

_____

_____

_____

_____

_____

_____

_____

_____

_____

_____

_____

_____

_____

_____

How can I create a regular habit of celebrating my growth and honoring my progress?

_____

_____

_____

_____

_____

_____

_____

_____

_____

_____

_____

_____

_____

_____

_____

_____

_____

_____

_____

Emotions Wheel

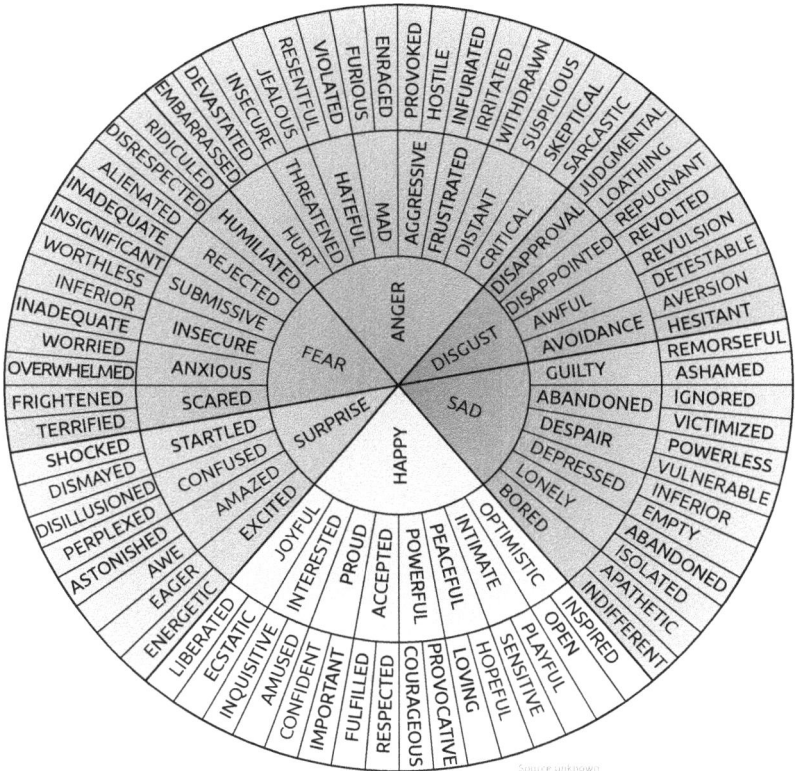

Source unknown

Closing Reflections

_____

_____

_____

_____

_____

_____

_____

_____

_____

_____

_____

_____

_____

_____

_____

_____

_____

_____

_____

_____

_____

_____

_____

_____

_____

_____

_____

_____

_____

_____

_____

_____

_____

_____

_____

_____

_____

_____

_____

_____